Miracle of Astrology

Miracle of Astrology

MALA GANGULY

Copyright © 2025 by Mala Ganguly.

The content contained within this book may not be reproduced, duplicated or transmitted without direct written permission from the author or the publisher.

Under no circumstances will any blame or legal responsibility be held against the publisher, or author, for any damages, reparation, or monetary loss due to the information contained within this book, either directly or indirectly.

This book is copyright protected. It is only for personal use. You cannot amend, distribute, sell, use, quote or paraphrase any part, or the content within this book, without the consent of the author or publisher.

ISBN 979-8-89965-698-9 (print)

Cover art © Mala Ganguly
Cover and interior design by Maureen Forys,
Happenstance Type-O-Rama

ACKNOWLEDGEMENTS & GRATITUDE

Sharifah Rosso

Raj Chatterjee

Dr Ratul Chatterjee

Subir Adhikari

Maninder Sethi Sagar

Tina Rahman

Alina Romanova

Mrs Atrei Banerjee

Mr Shubhra Banerjee

Mr Azhar Hameed

I also wish to express my gratitude to Leslie Schneider who graciously came forward when needed to give me a hand in writing this book and to give tribute to my precious uncle Chatterjee.

FOREWORD

This book is a tribute to my beloved astrologer Sree Satyen Chatterjee who deepened my life by generously and selflessly sharing his skills and insights. I benefited tremendously from our years of interaction. Meetings with him started as occasional, but as life went on, we sustained a natural connection which spanned decades. Due to his insightful guidance and warmth, I was able to overcome many difficult stormy times. He was such a giving person, but I never felt that I gave enough back to him except my love, respect and appreciation. I decided to write this book as an act of gratitude and genuine affection. I also wanted to describe how astrology came into my life through my uncle. I invite you to take a retrospective journey into one of the most meaningful relationships in my life.

INTRODUCTION

The Rainy Day

It was a rainy day. For my whole life, whenever I go back to that scene, I still almost can hear that rain. It was a beautiful rainy day. I was practicing figure drawing at the Kolkata Government Art Museum. There, art students were allowed to draw the statues at a special time reserved just for them. At this time, our former next-door neighbor, whom we called "Manju auntie", or "Jethima"', unexpectedly showed up, wearing a printed cotton kota sari, beautiful in mauve and off-white. She headed straight for me and said with a big smile, "Let's go, you are coming to my home." This was a turning point in my life. I thought my father was to pick me up, but apparently Jethima had been to his office, and he had suggested I go with her that evening. I remember very clearly; she gave me some jalmuri and tea. We sat together for a while. Who knew that this fifth floor of Jethima's house on Chaurangi Road would bring a dramatic change into my life. As I waited for my Baba to bring me home from her house later, a man arrived at the home and I heard Jethima say to the gentleman, "*Esho* (come in), there is someone I would like to introduce you to." This is how the story begins. It was 1979.

Jethima said to this man, who I came to know as Mr.Satyen Chatterjee, "Please read Mala's palm. I really want her to understand your gifts." This businessman was also an expert in Vedic astrology and could see a lot from looking at one's palm. I knew nothing of these things.

By looking at my hand, he said, "This girl will go overseas, she will be going to foreign countries." When he said that, Jethima said, "What is so remarkable about that, she has been going abroad since she was ten." "She will be going alone", he replied. "Alone?" Jethima asked. "Yes", he confirmed, "on her own."

He continued, "Yes, she will go soon and travel on her own. She will try to come back to Kolkata in two months but won't be able to, her journey home will be interrupted. She will have to return to the States and at that time she will stay a little more than ten months. Her future is overseas, not in India. Eventually she will be living in foreign countries. Her destiny is to go abroad, and I see that it will be for a long time, permanently."

Aunt, auntie in Bengali

Introduction

I reacted by not believing this, as to leave Kolkata was simply too much to imagine. I was so much in love with the city, I was the last person to think this. I could never imagine living without my *phuchka* (pani puri), all the classical music conferences, learning music from Guruji, and my beloved fragrant flowers of spring, Arabian Jasmine, or *Moghra*. I ignored this statement by him and felt it was just too much to comprehend. Visiting abroad was perhaps okay, but to suggest I leave permanently, just after seeing my hand, was something I emphatically did not want to imagine. This is the first episode of this story. Although I didn't believe Chatterjee Uncle immediately, slowly it started to prove itself and sink in. It began to seem as though life was unfolding just as he had predicted. It seemed as clear as the equation two plus two equals four.

I used to spend so much time at Jethima's house painting and learning how to knit. Jethima was a fantastic sari designer, seamstress and craftsperson, having studied at the Government Art College. She was always sharing her love for these things with me. She used to take me to New Market and buy me guavas that I loved to eat, beautiful bangles, and dangling earrings (*jhumkas*), and always coming back from the shopping with all the goodies with *jueymala* (garlands made from jasmine blossoms). After that first encounter with Chatterjee Uncle I would meet him again several times in the next few weeks at Jethima's home, and he would never fail to ask to study my hand. He always brought me a jasmine mala and some treats to eat. Jethima and Chatterjee Uncle would take me with them as they shopped for ingredients at New Market for Chinese food and other dishes that we would make and eat together. She could make very tasty food such as biriyani as well, using very little oil. She was known in the community for these remarkable gifts. It was an exciting and special time, especially as I was not inclined to leave my house too often socially. I was curious and had interest in Chatterjee Uncle's predictions, but I didn't take them too seriously. Slowly, the three of us started to meet regularly on a frequent basis as we appreciated each other's company. My mind still remembers those special days with such fondness and gratitude. Chatterjee Uncle started reading my palm on a regular basis.

On one of the occasions when I was meeting Chatterjee Uncle and Jethima, as usually, I asked him insistently to read my palm. This time he said, "You are going to have a head injury in your older age (*Oh, ho buro Bayoshe Matha Phatbey)!*" he exclaimed. Did you have this kind of injury before?" I then recounted to him scene from when I was five, something I had practically forgotten about. I was playing with the daughter of a well-known Bengali theater and film personality Utpal Dutta who lived right across from us. We were both playing in front

INTRODUCTION

of their stairway. I had a fall and hit my head. I was bleeding, and this artist picked me up and took me home. The head injury Chatterjee Uncle referred to actually did take place when I was older in Los Angeles in 2018. It occurred to me only later that this was his prediction from decades earlier come true.

On one occasion, in April, Jethima and I met with Chatterjee Uncle, and after his regular study of my palm, he said something so interesting that I felt struck by its shimmering clarity. I had been speaking highly of a man who I had fallen in love with, praising his singing skills and musical talent, but felt very depressed as the relationship had not worked out. Chatterjee Uncle said with a gentle smile, "I understand that you are hurting and can see that from time to time you feel very down about your breakup. But why are you always feeling so disturbed about this person? You say you are in love with him, but it is a one-sided love." Then Chatterjee Uncle added a question, "Is this man in love with someone else who is close to the same height as he is, someone with the same astrological sign or same last name?" I listened with a sense of quiet wonder. He continued, "Actually, the breakup is to be a blessing in disguise as you will be much better off without him. That man may be nice, but he is not a good match for you. It is not a good indicator for your future. Although he is a beautiful singer, I don't see a very bright future in the music field for him. He will struggle very hard. You, on the other hand, have a fantastic future in music ahead of you and this similar aspiration can cause much tension. On top of this, he is not right for you astrologically. I feel it is time to start thinking of your own path now." He then turned to Jethima and said, "If she goes abroad as soon as the middle of next month, I would not be surprised."

He continued to look at my palm, "I see that some kind of devastating tragedy and crime has happened in your family. Partly due to that, I can see a big change will occur within the family." I was overwhelmingly struck by this as it was true. Just a short time before, my mother's immediate sister and her husband had been murdered in Kolkata. The children of this family were brought into our home by Baba to stay with us as their own immediate relatives had not cared to help out. Unbeknownst to me, my father had just purchased flight tickets for me and my sister to visit and learn from a great Indian musician in California who had offered to teach us during the summer. He had purchased tickets for both me and my sister for mid-May, but as my sister couldn't go, I would be traveling alone. This prediction of my traveling alone was exactly as I was told when my palm was viewed at that first blessed meeting with Chatterjee Uncle. I

Father in Bengali

really had my trust in his capacities develop more deeply when my flight was booked by my Baba* for May 15th. I wondered how much more middle of the month that could be! At this point, my mind sensed I could begin to have some trust in his astrological predictions. Before that point, I had been fairly casual in my response. I still had questions about the upcoming experiences of my solo trip abroad to the U.S. via London. I thought to myself, "Was he going to be predicting all my movements in life? No! How can that be?" Reflecting further though, I started realizing that this was something very real. And it was to be the first striking prediction for me of many by this great man.

Chatterjee Uncle was giving guidance not only to me, but he was helping other family members as well. My brother has always been of sanyasi type. When my father was working at British Airways, many people would come and have a drink with him for various reasons. My Dada* didn't like to see my father involved in such unsavory social interactions, where much social manipulation seemed to be happening. My father had also been very hard on Dada, and his anger toward him had built up. About 1977, Dada all of a sudden said he was leaving, but only by leaving a note saying he was renouncing the family. My mother then was hospitalized with

---

Elder brother in Bengali

an ulcer partly due to this situation with her only son had left without any communication.

My father then took an interest in Chatterjee Uncle and his astrology expertise. He was so concerned for my mother and her health with this situation. He asked me to request Chatterjee Uncle to visit so he could talk with him and look at his chart. Chatterjee Uncle told us, "Give me a little time. I will come back to you in two days". Baba could not sleep and kept waiting by the gate looking for him to come back. In two days, Chatterjee Uncle returned to the house and said, "No worries, your son will be back. Tell him to wear the gem stone *gomed* (in Bengali). Please ask him to wear this within a certain time frame. He himself will contact you and you will get the opportunity to tell him this. His life will work out for him in terms of work and connecting back to you." We came to know that Dada was staying at my mother's Boro Mama*'s house, he then told us that Dada had gone in uncle's house in Ahmedabad. "Be patient, as we must let him know that at least his mother needs to see him as she is not keeping well." We all went to Hemant Kumar's house in Mumbai where we had planned to meet up with my brother. He was so thin, did pranam to mother and father and said, "I will come back when I can, please don't push me." At this time, my father told Dada that the

---

* *Elder brother in Bengali*

astrologer had asked him to wear the stone during a certain time and that we were hoping he would come back whenever he felt.

The ring was made ready so that, when Dada finally came home in Kolkata, we gave it to him to wear. My mother did a small puja that day with the ring. We all went to Birmingham where my father had found a possible training for Dada that could help him. Generally, in the past, Dada did not like to comply with my Baba's choices and help but this time he agreed. We all went with him to the UK to help him settle there. Dada completed the course and returned to us in Kolkata. He got a job immediately in Madhya Pradesh. My mother was relieved and could finally relax a bit knowing her son was no longer estranged and was doing ok.

UNFOLDING PREDICTIONS

So, right in the middle of May I headed to the U.S. alone as it was predicted by Chatterjee Uncle. After a short time in California, I became so restless without the usual busy activities of Kolkata and felt tired and bored without anything much to do. The person I stayed with was a little abusive too. My ticket to fly back to Kolkata was sitting with me so I decided to head home. The air ticket was via London, and when I reached there, I was picked up from the airport by my father's friend with whom I would stay for a day or so. He immediately announced with laughter that there was a new twist, and that instead of flying back to Kolkata as planned, I would be meeting my parents in London the next day. "Surprise, Mala!" he chuckled, as he was having fun with me. "You think you are heading to Kolkata but that is not the case. Be ready to head toward California again!" After my Baba arrived, he suggested that we would be traveling straight back to Los Angeles together since we were already halfway between both India and the U.S. He said we would see Disneyland, meet some family friends, and then finally head home to India. This was the interruption of my return journey to Kolkata that Chatterjee Uncle had so clearly envisioned at that remarkable first meeting just a few months before. The fact that I was returning to California made his next prediction realized.

After arriving, I was invited and then performed in several Indian events and concerts in Los Angeles during this time. Both listeners and concert organizers in the Bengali community insisted to my Baba that I should stay longer, and they would take care of me, assuring him that I would be presented in many of their cultural programs and Indian religious functions. These community members had a simple but good motivation wanting my help to sustain and develop Bengali culture and art here in the U.S. They requested my father to change the flight date and to have my visa extended with the idea that it would be fruitful to have for these cultural programs. My Baba agreed on my behalf, and yet, upon hearing this, I cried in protest of the decision. I did end up staying in the U.S. for exactly ten months more, performing frequently for concerts and pujas. Gradually, Chatterjee Uncle's predictions were unfolding, whether I liked it or not.

During this stay in L.A. the Bengali community had found that in addition to my musicianship as a vocalist and harmonium player, I was also an experienced visual artist. As such, I was very versatile in doing the creative artwork needed for the community's dance and drama productions. I filled my time with everything, from dressmaking to stage decorations and makeup, and found these activities very rewarding. It seemed like I covered every aspect of Bengali music and art. My early intense training in dance had also helped me understand the needs of these productions. As I began to stay on in the U.S., I felt very satisfied to share these skills and see some impact within the wider community.

MEETING A SPECIAL SOUL

Before I left India in 1980, Chatterjee Uncle had predicted presence of a person who would protect me and help me throughout my journey in the new country, and had described him physically. He said, "Whoever this person is, he will be extremely supportive to you. He would have a sharp nose and back brushed hair and would come later into your life. He would be over 45 years old, very caring, with broad shoulders, and a little taller than an average Bengali man." Little did I know, this person would become my soulmate, a person who was all relationships in one. A once in a lifetime connection. I felt fully comfortable with him first as a human, a friend and a noble character. He seemed like the kind of person who could rescue me if I ever needed.

Our initial meeting happened at one concert where I was invited along with my family (parents and sister), only several days after we came back to the U.S. from London. When I first met him, I felt like I had known him for years, and I didn't know how that could be. I had no idea he was the person that Uncle had spoken about. I then found out that he was an extremely talented person and an amazing music lover with a strong artistic sensibility. And, most importantly to me, had very caring nature. He was a giving person not only to individuals, but to both the whole Bengali and wider Indian community. To me, he was supportive and concerned, and like a rock. He stood out from among all the other music aficionados I was meeting, and his nature was one which I felt a deep affinity. He later told me that he could not sleep the first time he heard me sing as he had been so moved and overwhelmed with the impact it had made on him.

Even my music career was developing due to this friend and protector of mine. The initial concert I performed in L.A. for wider audience also happened in 1980. It was a starting point to my professional vocal career. At that time, Punjabi community was much more active in terms of culture than Bengali. Prashun ji suggested that I should broaden my horizon and start performing not only for Bengali audience. I had been given an opportunity to sing in one house by one music connoisseur from Punjab. This man had always felt that no non-Punjabi should sing their music as the accent and voice would not be close. "Singing a ghazal with Bengali accent I don't even want to hear! That's like singing in Urdu with a rasgoula* in the mouth," he said. "Just listen to her voice and singing!" Prashun ji proudly proclaimed. Prashun ji knew I was at the beginning of my deeper study of Urdu but still said, "Even if the pronunciation is not perfect just listen to her voice!" The Punjabi organizer Mr. Singh kept my program, but I was just one of many singers that day. My turn came at the end of the program, around 2 a.m. This was my first concert here on my first trip. I sang for 2 hours until 4 a.m. It was a total success. I sang many ghazals, geets, and Bollywood film numbers. At that time, ghazals were very much appreciated and in great demand. I had a big repertoire of this genre of songs, which the community valued highly. Prashun ji, who felt I was someone special for his life, was so proud and proved to the organizer that his discernment of my artistry was correct. As it turned out, the organizer invited me the next day to sing in his radio program.

After staying in America this first time, and after extending my visitor's visa, the Bengalis bade me a formal farewell by offering an official "goodbye" concert program, and then I left for India. This first stay in the U.S. was exactly 10 months (1½ months then London then back), just as Chatterjee Uncle had predicted when I was in Kolkata before I left.

An ethnic Indian milk based sweet, flavoured with rosewater and syrop

He had also predicted that after staying in the U.S. for two months, I would go back soon. That did happen but as it happened, I left the U.S. after just 1½ months and went to India via London. His insights were beginning to have quite a profound influence on me and seemed more and more to be a call of destiny.

In 1982 I told my Baba I hoped to travel abroad and he replied, "Yes, British Airways is not going to continue to give free tickets as they have done, it is good to take advantage of their policies until they are no longer available." He asked, "Do you want to travel with me?" and I said, "Yes, I would love to." That year I misplaced my passport though. I remembered that Chatterjee Uncle had read my chart and said that from July there will be an astrological position where the stars will make it difficult for me to travel. "You will have obstacles which you cannot avoid."

Overnight Baba went to the police station and applied for a new passport for me. That was the time I was in a serious depression. The suburb we lived in then was Rajpur. It was outside Kolkata and simply was not for me. I was looking for a place that could be better so thought about giving another country a try. We decided to go to London and then, perhaps, on to the U.S. but we needed a visa for that trip. Chatterjee Uncle told my Baba, "Don't go to any consulate for any visa purposes now. At least, try to do so only after the 4th of October. The alignment of the stars places her ability to get the visa only after the 4th. After arriving in London, we had planned to go to the consulate for our U.S. visa. But my Baba had a cold and bronchitis which he had even before traveling and this had gotten worse. For that reason, he wanted to go to the immigration office right away after arriving in London on the 1st. He didn't like the idea of waiting around. I kept asking my Baba to please wait until the 4th or even after. He became intense and said, "Why doesn't this astrologer think about me? I want to leave London and he wants me to wait here in this terrible climate, not feeling well. This is absurd." But even with that he decided to stay. We went to the immigration office on the 4th. "Why do you want to go the U.S.? Are you planning to get a job?" the officer asked. He continued, "Why are you carrying U.S. dollars? If not planning to stay, why do you need to carry this money?" My Baba explained that we might need it in case of emergency and we wanted to visit Disneyland before we go back to India. Baba then added that he kept it just in case. The officer gave us the visa and asked us to raise our right hands and promise not to take any American job over there. "You are just going to visit." Then he stamped the passport. I got the visa as uncle predicted by the 4th of October.

Before coming back to the U.S. a second time, a letter arrived to me in Kolkata from Prashun ji mentioning how he missed me and valued my singing. He showed much concern and care for my career over several pages of the letter.

FIRST YEARS OF IMMIGRATION

During my first visits to U.S., whenever I was in Los Angeles, I would stay with a loving Bengali family. The whole family had become very attached to me. The lady of the house needed me for any help that I could provide. I used to cook for everyone there and help in other areas as well. While living there though, I became concerned that if I continued staying on, I would lose my very presence, my music, my focus, and my career. While staying at the house, I was working with the local community by providing so much service that after a while I felt lost. Much of my time was preoccupied with the daily activities that were nonmusical, trying to just maintain a roof over my head. Nothing was moving in the direction I had hoped and it was not fruitful for my career.

One Bengali dancer and her husband had become admirers during this time. She also was very upset that I was neglecting my talents and skills as I helped others for their achievements, including helping in one person's home, and also within the community when they needed assistance in organizing concerts. She had written a letter to my father telling him that in the U.S. I was avoiding my career and not utilizing my talent properly and, essentially, not thinking of my career or my future. She was extremely pleased with my singing and saw my potential as a performing artist. She mentioned how I helped create and organize artistic endeavors like Bengali dance dramas and music concerts, but I wasn't involved as a performer. This dancer saw the injustice of this for me. My father wrote to Prashun ji as he had become very upset and said he would come to California to rescue me.

I also wrote to Chatterjee Uncle in early 1983 saying that I was feeling devastated and that I should move back to India as there was nothing there for me. I had even started to make one suitcase ready for the move back to Kolkata. Frustration was a constant companion. After receiving my letter, Chatterjee Uncle wrote me back and said, "Do not give up your hope, you must stay in the U.S., do not come to India. Doors will open for you there. Stick to the plan of staying, even if you don't like it. Before July 9th, you will get one offer to move out from where you are staying. It will be an important milestone."

As it happened, near July 9th, I was invited to sing a concert at a farewell party of a local Muslim and music connoisseur Mr. Miyan. A family friend's wife in the community had suggested my name for this party. She was the wife of Prashun ji, an active Bengali musical and community member. He was someone who played tabla with me on occasion as well. At the event presented by Mr. Miyan, Prashun ji's wife was also present. She had come to know from Prashun ji that I had lost hope in my present circumstances. She came up to me and offered me a room in their home. She said I could teach there beginning with their family members. My Baba wrote to Prashun ji that he was coming from India on a certain date to help me move from my present house to the home of Prashun ji and his family. After the move and before Baba returned to India, he requested Prashun ji to help me to move out to my own rented place as soon as possible. He wanted me to be self-sufficient. Baba came to L.A. and helped me to move and, eventually, after two months or so I could then find a place for myself. It happened in 1983. Having a student visa (which Prashun ji helped me to get), I enrolled in East LA Community College. I began to be an independent person, with roommates sharing the rent. That year, I began singing more and getting an increased number of concerts. I was singing solos as well as accompaniment for Kathak. Now the ball really started rolling in terms of my career. After 1985 invitations to different concerts and performances became even more abundant.

GOD'S GLANCE

This story took place at the end of 1983. When I was only starting my independent life, I was scared inside. I wrote to Chatterjee Uncle to express my feelings, and his answer was, "Just pray to God, and you will be rescued, God will help you anyway."

The house I moved into had two roommates from China, Easy and his wife Joy. They asked me to pay $195 for the room per month. The day I moved in, I was asked to pay immediately. Easy said, "Hi Mala, I need $195 for the room tonight. Plus a deposit of $195. You must give it to me tonight!" I replied, "Of course, I will bring it after my concert." Easy kept insisting for the money before I left for the program that evening where I would earn $150. I was unaware of the tradition of needing to pay the first and the last month rent. "Of course, I will pay you as soon as I come back from my show tonight." In the back of my mind, I thought it would work out. As I was getting ready to leave the house for the concert, Easy again demanded, "You must pay the $195 for this month and the deposit now." I had no choice, though, but to leave, with the hope of earning a portion of money needed. My mood was so off after going through this. When I arrived at the concert, I hoped I could manage. I saw that it was mostly a Punjabi crowd. I started singing Punjabi songs which a dear friend had suggested I work on the preceding weeks. I was not worrying about the money as the show must go on. I started the performance and after 4 or 5 songs the mehfil* was warming up. In the back of my mind, I was still thinking, "What will I do about the rent?" I remembered hearing from Hemant Kumar that when he was performing in London the Punjabi people started throwing money on his harmonium. That same thing started happening that night. And then, the more I sang upbeat numbers, the more the crowd went wild. And when I sang the two Punjabi songs, people went crazy in appreciation and showed this with their respectful habit of throwing money onto the harmonium. I didn't pay attention to the money while singing but afterwards the tabla player came up to me holding all the cash, plus the $150 check from the host, and I came home after the show with exactly $408. It felt like God was rescuing me from that monetary need for the rent on that night and

---

* *An evening of poetry or concert of Hindustani classical music and dance taking place in a private space and performed for a small audience; derived from Arabic word meaning gathering, assembly.*

telling me to sleep well. It was the best night's sleep I had had in a long time. In the morning, when I gave the rent, it was the start of my musical journey as a performer.

All in all between 1980 and 1985 I travelled to India 3 or 4 times. I hadn't yet decided to stay in the U.S. permanently. Even my father could not believe that I was going to live there. But Chatterjee Uncle had always seen that I would be growing and glowing in this faraway country.

VISIT TO INDIA IN 1985

I became ill (with a hernia) and went back to India in May 1985. I gave up my apartment in L.A. and left. It was a real turning point. Once there, I went naturally and immediately to Chatterjee Uncle. He again saw my chart and hand. He told me, "This time when you go back you will see a big difference in your career there." He gave me two special stones to wear. He said that in five years time someone would come into my life and disturb me, and these stones would help. "With Prashun ji you will have a true understanding and this relationship will grow. Also, when you return back to the U.S., you will receive a gift of something like "a chariot" with four wheels. And this will be gifted to you by a non-Hindu." I thought he was kidding, as it was such a large amount of money that would be spent. "Who would do such a thing?" I asked him in a surprised manner. "I am telling you only what I am seeing", he replied. His prediction about my career was soon revealed. Just after he spoke to me, I received two letters from the

U.S., from a Kathak and Bharat Natyam dancer each with two different offers for me to perform in L.A. but both were on the same date in August. Both were major festivals with esteemed guest artists for each Pt Birju Maharaj and Pt Ravi Shankar. I accepted both offers and managed to go to both locations on the same night.

1985 was a significant year in one more sense. At that point, I was confused, deciding whether to stay in the U.S. or not, and feeling insecure because of this uncertainty. I started doing a very wrong thing in my life, chewing tobacco and paan*. I used to consume up to 30 paans a day! I was also drinking Californian wine, not a glass during the dinner, but always till I get tipsy, which was totally incompatible with my health problems (hernia). When I was talking to Chatterjee Uncle, I asked him if everything was ok with my chart. He told me, "Yes, everything is fine. But I see that there is something you are doing excessively in your life. After all, you are an adult, and I do not want to interfere in your personal affairs, but I think it is not proper for a young girl like you to consume alcohol and paan." Here, Chatterjee Uncle acted a role of a spiritual guide. He was very gentle and considerate, not putting any pressure on me. But due to his influence, when I

---

* *A mixture of betel nut, herbs and often tobacco, wrapped in a betel leaf.*

came back to the U.S. from India, I totally quit my bad habits. I am so thankful to Chatterjee Uncle that I was stopped in a right time.

During this my visit to India our family got one more gift from Chatterjee Uncle. At some point, I saw a girl coming to visit our family's house. I came to know that my brother was seeing her, and it was a serious connection. He was taking time to decide and seemed hesitant about marrying over the two years they were seeing each other. Earlier, this girl had expressed her feelings to me about my brother and seemed determined that he was the only person for her. I asked Chatterjee Uncle to take a look at my brother's chart as soon as possible. He asked me why I was in such a rush. On the day Uncle came over, I remember, it was very stormy and rainy. He looked at the chart and my brother's palm. My brother was in Kolkata because of my visit from America. Chatterjee Uncle said, "He has a very strong timing, or "yog", for the date of this wedding. If it does happen, it will happen this month, before mid-July. If it doesn't happen this month, then it may not ever happen." In a few days' time Dada's friend visited my father one evening and gave him a message, saying that the girl's father wanted to meet with him, suggesting that the delay in marriage between his daughter and my brother was becoming much too long. This was a sudden change in his attitude, as he had not appeared interested at all in discussing this before. That day he talked about the wedding arrangements and asked if my father was serious about seeing it happen. My father said he was. It was settled and after just one week, on July 9th, Dada got married. As this was very close to the time of my brother's leaving back to Madhya Pradesh, the marriage happened quickly. Again, another miracle vision of Chatterjee Uncle, this time related to my brother's destiny.

COMING BACK TO U.S. IN 1985 FOR A LONG 31 YEARS

This time I started liking the freedom of being away from home and doing something on my own. My music and performances were being more and more appreciated here. Ten different families in the community asked me to stay with them and wanted me to extend my visa. I performed in many concerts and a variety of venues. I was convinced to continue staying in America after witnessing Prashun ji's genuine feelings and career support.

I landed in the U.S. on August 15, 1985, exactly on India's Independence day, and this my stay was colored with the joy of my independence and freedom. On arrival I immediately started to prepare for the program, where I had been invited during my visit to India. One night with both legends of music and dance in the two different halls! In the first program, I sang with Pt. Maharaj in attendance and then in the second, I sang an invocation in raga

Hamsadhwani in front of Pt. Ravi Shankarji. He listened with enthusiasm and said that I had "such a sweet voice".

During this time, Dr. Khan and his wife were taking lessons from me, and they offered me a place in their home. They had already been so hospitable when I had been ill before going to India. I was staying with the family (1986) while still looking for a place of my own. Prashun ji again actively helped me find a new apartment to rent. Around this time, I found Pauline who was the Kathak master and Pt. Chitresh Das' student. Pauline and I decided to share a house together, along with Pauline's teenage daughter Lisa. As I walked into Pauline's house, I immediately smelled incense, which made me feel right at home. There were three bedrooms there, one for each of us. I stayed. Soon, I got busier and busier with engagements of Kathak accompaniment as well as solo vocal performances.

At this time, I was looking for a car so I could drive to my college. Dr. Khan and his wife surprised me one day with a car (Or is this a chariot as Chatterjee Uncle predicted?). He wanted to give me a new car, but upon further thought he realized that, as a new driver, I might be better off with a used one.

Also, before going back to India I applied for the green card and it was approved in the special category for a multi-dimensional artist. I only got the actual green card after ten years. Chatterjee Uncle had made a curious prediction and stated emphatically, "Whoever sponsors you, that person will be a non-Hindu." Even after having the approval document in hand, he again said it will still be delayed. "Do not leave the country, stay where you are until you have the card in hand," he insisted. Just as he had predicted, it was still delayed another two and a half years after this. In the process the immigration department had lost my passport and the I-94 card, creating another delay. Additionally, my lawyer was told to get lost for not bringing his Bar card when he was inquiring about the status of the green card.

I remember wanting to go to Mumbai for the green card interview at the U.S. Consulate, but Chatterjee Uncle emphatically said I should not go. This was the typical place to do an interview. My friends also thought I should go and reminded me of the possible music opportunities in Mumbai, and suggested that being there could be good all around.

One day, when I was in a restaurant in Los Angeles, a friend, Mr. Modi, walked in, holding an Indian—American newspaper, and exclaimed, "Good news for you, Mala! A new rule has passed in the government in the U.S. in which you can get your green card without traveling abroad to do the interview. You can now do it right here in the U.S.!" After hearing the new immigration rule, my father said, "If you have to give a service fee to the immigration department (part of the new rule) to do the interview here, I will help pay this, no worries. You don't need to leave the country." Throughout this time Chatterjee Uncle had kept insisting all along that I do not leave the country. My father was in the U.S. visiting me at this time. A short time before, upon traveling from L.A. to Canada where he had some businesses and upon his return to L.A. in 1993, he fell sick and needed surgery, something which was best done in the U.S.

All of this happened during the time I might have been in Mumbai if Chatterjee Uncle had not insisted that I stay back in Los Angeles. He had said, "You are already established here in the field and career wise, and for that reason, your difficulties here will be less by staying." Others, I knew though, were impatient with uncle's insistence that it would be better for me to stay. "Mumbai is the place," Prashun ji and others would say, "for a singer like you, with the film industry and other musical opportunities right there." It turned out though, that it was very important that I could stay and help my father with his surgery. "You have to wait somewhere anyway, why not to wait here in the U.S. In your astrological chart, star-wise even though you have been given the green card approval, I see it will be arai bocho (it will be 2½ years), before you receive the card in hand."

After waiting for the green card for years and trying every job with the hope of getting a sponsor (teaching music, for example, at the Vedanta Society in L.A.), I finally got the card in hand on June 4th, 1995 (exactly 2½ years later as predicted). Chatterjee Uncle kept insisting that I be careful with documentation as delays would result in it being not managed, as he could see that dilemma with paperwork would be a problem throughout much of my life. This included huge documentation for visa issues and my passport and I-94 getting lost in the immigration department.

My turning point was coming in 1995. A new start, a fresh start. Chatterjee Uncle had seen that.

MY BELOVED JETHIMA COMES TO ME

Along with the green card journey there was another miracle story that comes with it. In 1994 I had both the challenge and privilege of bringing my beloved Jethima, who at that time was a 74-year-old dying cancer patient, from India to the U.S. She had been going through a very serious illness since 1978, and doctors told her that, because of her age, they would be unable to operate on her. It had been predicted by them she would live only fifteen days and yet, after coming to the U.S., she lived another 16 years. This was my wonderful auntie Jethima in whose house I had met my astrologer Uncle. As close friends, we made a kind of triangle, all of us of different generations. She had always wanted to visit America, but Chatterjee Uncle always suggested she wait. "You will have a chance to go overseas much later, but not just now. Be patient." "When will I go, when will it be my turn?" she would often ask him, after seeing that my destiny to travel had been predicted by him in my chart. She always wanted to leave Kolkata, because typical society in India used to point a finger to her as a working woman, and also because of her intelligent, independent, and outgoing nature, something not seen among those who were widowed. She did not follow the typical conventions. Her son's wife and family were especially critical of her, and her son chose to align with them. The difficulties she experienced with her son became her pressure point and the main reason she wanted to leave. She had raised her only son alone, as her husband died, and gave him a beautiful marriage with the person he wanted to marry. Her daughter-in-law was a doctor, and her son also became a doctor. Later, Jethima's granddaughter was in the medical field too. And yet, disturbingly, they abandoned her during her sickness, not helping during the worst part of her illness, leaving her in the cold during her hospital stays and times when she needed convalescent care.

Once I heard Jethima again ask Chatterjee Uncle, "When will I go then, when I am ready to die?" Chatterjee Uncle said half-seriously, *"Oh, dore nau (who knows, Bengali)?* Just consider that it may happen. You never quite know when. But the truth is, no one has the power to make you die. You have the strength to live."

During a period in 1994, Jethima developed more serious health issues. She was losing weight and was in and out of hospital several times. Around this time, Chatterjee Uncle said to me on the phone from India, "If she can reach America by the 25th of December 1994, then she will have a chance to live more. She will get treatment there in the U.S." I spoke with Prashun ji hoping that we could do something for her. "What can we do? Can we bring her here and the doctor's might be able to save her?" I had no idea how serious her illness was then. Once she arrived though, I understood, and the challenge to manage and help her became very real. Prashun ji, as my best friend, empathetically offered the idea of bringing her as a visitor. He prepared the visa work and personally sponsored her. With her savings she bought a ticket and came to the U.S., landing here on Christmas eve. A few days before, my father had come to L.A. in order to have surgery. He had recovered and was about to go back to India soon, on the 1st of January. For five months I had been taking care of my father, and now my journey with my Auntie's recovery was about to begin. We all went to pick her up from the airport, including my father. I could not recognize Auntie or find her on the wheelchair, she was that thin. My father asked how the airline personnel could even let her on the plane, someone so obviously ill. "How could they even allow her?" he would say.

He was also concerned that my finances could not manage such an intense situation as this. He knew I only had money coming in from music.

But amazingly that coming year, in 1995, so many musical bookings came my way including a Nike commercial (which became #3 among the top 10 commercials that year), the soundtrack for a CBS Christmas Box movie, a JC Penny commercial and many more. This was also predicted by Chatterjee Uncle who told me that soon I would have a second source of income. We were fine financially after these engagements. Father said, "How can you continue to manage this person, what about your own mother? She has needs too." "She is getting treatment now, don't talk like that", I said. "If you want to send Mom here I will be glad to have her. I will sleep in the garage and give her my bed." Then he apologized and understood where my motivation was from, how pure was my intention. UC Medical started treating Jethima by operating on her for a full hysterectomy to take out the tumor. Because it was cancer, she had chemotherapy.

Chatterjee Uncle was comforting me saying, "You will be helped out." I could not believe it, but after some time she received "Medi-cal", and all the health benefits needed without cost from the California state government. I only had to help with expenses for lodging and food. My father saw later how she had recovered well. Chatterjee Uncle also had always said how she would recover and look better, would be back to a healthy weight and beautiful expression. This happened.

Throughout this particular time, my music and art were my inner support and made me smile, helping me to cope. Auntie was also creative during this time, using her imagination to paint saris and other fabrics, and pursuing embroidery and knitting. She would give away her artistically painted fabric pieces to the nurses and medical staff. It kept her busy. Later, Auntie developed blood clot in her foot, and Chatterjee Uncle said, "She is going through a sun sign (Ravi dasha) and she still has some years to live, so don't worry, she will recover." "How do you know?" she asked. He said that it would happen, he had a strong feeling. A Thai doctor working at the UC center attended to her and inserted a green filter on her thighs that prevented the clot from being a danger.

In 1995, on several occasions, Chatterjee Uncle predicted that after five years some significant changes would occur in my life. "I will tell you when the time comes closer", he would say. Then just as he predicted, after five years, in 2000, changes did occur. The landlady whose home Jethima and I were staying in, gave us an immediate eviction notice. Chatterjee Uncle said, "You may not realize it now, but this is actually a blessing in disguise. Don't worry about it at all." I was surprised. "What?" I exclaimed. "They are giving an eviction notice? Where will we go? I don't have money to buy a home." "A property purchase will be happening", he replied. I was unsure of this, though, and said, "That will be a miracle, I don't have money saved for such a thing." He then said that when looking at Jethima's chart, it predicted that later in life she would have property and some unexpected fortune would happen to help her purchase it. "Just take some ginger and water (*ada jol khey lago*)," he said, expressing the familiar Bengali phrase. "It will happen, just get to work. For this home purchase, I see a non-Hindu coming to be of some kind of help." He mentioned that there could be help from a Hindu also, but initially he was distinct in his vision that a non-Hindu would be coming forward to help us. I had been looking for a place for Jethima and me together for a long time but had not been able to find anything that I could afford. I had practically buried myself in my car under all the real estate newspapers while looking for a place. I would search diligently through every ad with homes for sale.

One day, two different real estate agents called, both with a house available. I wasn't sure which one to go and see. One agent had a home ready with very tiny rooms, but he insisted in a very pushy way that it was great, because it had a big avocado tree. On the other line there was a different agent who had found a good condo at an affordable price. He asked if there was any way I could come to the property within 15 minutes. I went with that one as it was closer in distance, and had three bedrooms and

2 bathrooms, and was less expensive than the other one (although no avocado tree!). It turned out the house I went to see had an address with a number "6" in it, which is a number I always look for as my number, as it has seemed connected throughout my life to important things. My half-Italian music student around this time asked me to dinner and insisted that I take some funds from her savings CD in the bank and simply handed me a check for $10,000. Some wealthy friends in the Bengali community came together and funded the remaining $10,000 balance for the down payment for a new home. They all helped me find this condo which we would eventually buy. Chatterjee Uncle requested me to do a worship or puja before we initially entered. This was the beginning of 2001. Jethima and I finally had a good sleep as we had no concerns about being evicted for the first time in a long period. It was a miracle to get Chatterjee Uncle's prediction, stating that we would own a house and it was a great heavenly feeling to sleep in this house. I managed to pay the mortgage for this condo for nine years, giving some solace especially to Jethima. It was in her chart that she would own a home and could relax in the shade of a roof over her head. My chart showed a different outcome and destiny in terms of my house when the recession of 2008 and 2009.

Near the time we were buying a house, I developed health problems. In the years leading up to

1999 there were seven months in which Chatterjee Uncle said to me occasionally that although he saw no other problems, he did see that I would lose blood for no obvious reason. When I was released from the hospital after having surgery for this issue, I told him how relieved I was to be out and home. He said, "You still have some more things to do". I asked, "What else?" Then I came to know that a tumor was forming during the ultrasound for the bleeding issue.

In October 2001 I was in the middle of preparing for the hysterectomy surgery, when I came back from the Minneapolis concert performance and broke my ankle. When the doctor saw my x-ray, he exclaimed, "What a nasty fracture!" I had foot surgery for six broken bones and I had to heal from that. I was on orthopedic boots. I had to be very careful on the wheelchair and later the walker.

After the doctors set my ankle, I was resting for two or three months, even with orthopedic boots I kept singing. One day I spoke with Chatterjee Uncle saying that my pain from endometriosis was less and that maybe I needn't do the advised surgery. He said, "No, you go ahead and do the surgery. You have to do it. Please, do it before July," he insisted. I said, "Kaku*, there is only two weeks before July. But let's see if I can find a better gynecologist." I

---

* *Uncle*

asked Dr. Khan. He suggested an Egyptian woman named Dr. Ragab. I immediately drove to Torrance where the appointment was, while having to take pain killers to get in the car.

She said that I must do the surgery soon, but she didn't see any beds available at the hospital. I insisted that it should happen before July. She said, "What, why?" I answered, "Because my Astrologer Uncle said it must be." She asked, "Do you believe in these things?" I said, "Yes, I do," emphatically. She said, "Okay let's see what I can do." She found a bed in a small hospital and scheduled the surgery for June 29th. After the surgery she said, that the endometriosis caused the inflammation that was touching all the other organs, and if we had waited another week, I could not have safely done this surgery.

Only 3 weeks after that major surgery a great show at California Plaza, L.A., was scheduled. I was still feeling weak, but no way I was ready to cancel that show. I decided to seek the advice of my Chatterjee Uncle. Considering my chart, he told me, "Mala, time is allowing you to do it, so do it!" These words became a great support to me and made me confident, and I never regretted that I found strength to go on. What a great event it was! A big open-air stage, Sunday, sold-out crowd, and the audience was not only Indian, but mostly American.

In 2005 I broke another ankle, this time the doctor exclaimed, trying to humor me, "Oh, you have a matching fracture!" Again my trauma synchronized with a big concert, this time at Paul Getti Museum. I walked to the stage holding someone's hand as I was in the orthopedic boot. This performance was also a success—it was a sold-out, the audience was very receptive, and despite the concert was short it sounded that people wanted more.

When I broke my ankle for the second time, my student Bina who had just begun taking lessons in the last three weeks somehow loved me from the first day. We had become very close. By the end of the third week of her lessons she got a phone call from a common friend of ours asking, "Did you know Mala broke her other ankle and is in the hospital?" Bina jumped and thought, "How was Mala going to manage?" Bina came to the hospital and said, "Come, Mala, let's go to my home." She picked me up and took me to her home, which was almost an hour and a half away. Eventually her kindness turned out to be a blessing to her as she became introduced to Chatterjee Uncle then. She was struggling in general and had green card issues. Because of her loving nature, she took me to her home to get on my feet again and just get better. And during this time Chatterjee Uncle gave her the benefit of his insights. While getting introduced to her, I got to meet Mina, Bina's sister. She had a story where she was taking care of an elderly person with an in-home health care group. While I was recovering from my ankle injury, I was able to meet her sister on the phone with Mina also on the call. Then, later, as I was going to the hospital with Bina's help, we stopped at Mina's. There I saw a similar situation, a divorced woman with unsuccessful marriages. Bina and Mina were interested in Chatterjee Uncle's predictions. They asked if he would do their charts. Bina wanted to know when she would get her green card and if her husband would help or if this would never happen. It had already been 4 years. We sat in the car in the moonlight. It was a beautiful night as the light of the moon shone on the sandy terrain of Palmdale. We also appreciated spending time away from her house. Chatterjee Uncle replied to the sister's questions about their charts, "You are almost there. I see that this doctor you are married to will help with the green card. Do not lose the opportunity and do not get frustrated. Just hold on. Keep on where you are staying." She heard this and said, "No, no, uncle, I can barely manage this life here! It's so very tiring!" He then responded, "Please be patient, don't rush or make any impulsive decisions about it." Chatterjee Uncle had mentioned that even if it doesn't happen right away, she needed to wait until the next year. Although it was just a few months away, Bina was impatient to leave her current situation and go to her daughter in Canada. The New Year came, and she went to the lawyer and they went over to INS, but they found papers missing; nothing happened. Then Chatterjee Uncle said, "Please, wait until April." Right around her birthday in the month of April she got her green card.

Mina then had her chart read. She had no home and was divorced. Her kids were in Bangladesh. She was taking care of an older person for her work. Chatterjee Uncle said, "Did your sister Mina have a near death experience ever?" Bina said, "Yes, she had a terrible car accident and was in a coma. I took care of her during this time. She had physical therapy and recovered though she still has some back problems." Chatterjee Uncle said, "That matched what I had seen." He continued, "She would face an opportunity to get some huge financial gift, not an inheritance. Where, I cannot tell, I am not God." Mina then asked when this would happen. Chatterjee Uncle said to wait another three or four years, to just hang on. It turned out that the elderly person that Mina was caring for wrote Mina into her will as a great appreciation for her help and left her a big property, which normally does not happen. Who leaves property to a caregiver when not all the people are able to give it to their own kids? Mina kept the house for a while and then sold it to have some resources to travel back and forth to Bangladesh and to start a business.

Just after my surgery for a hysterectomy and then with two broken ankles, I kept earning by teaching and singing. I moved from a wheelchair to crutches after about a month. Fortunately I was receiving royalties and performance fees (Music Circle, Paul Getty Museum) and was able to get along financially. Things became more difficult economically though, when students ebbed with their own financial issues, and costs for Auntie's medical care increased. Work opportunities grew less with the economic recession. I was still paying the mortgage until at one point I was offered a predatory loan and naively took it, not realizing the prevalent scams with mortgage refinancing. Chatterjee Uncle always said, "You will have problems and zigzags with money issues but you will overcome them. You will be fine monetarily. Some blessings will come from Jethima. Indirectly she will give some fortune ("Ashirbad diye jabe")."

One day after a music rehearsal, I drove back to Chhobi Di's during the very difficult time when Prashun ji was in a coma at the hospital. At that time, Monir and Indrani, friends of Chhobi di's were visiting her in her home. This was the day that Prashun ji passed away. I wasn't aware. Chhobi di said to Monir, "How can I possibly tell Mala? I just can't." Monir said he would tell me. When I entered the house, he said, "Come, Mala, let's all go for a ride." We went out for a drive in the car. Upon returning he told me in a very kind and quiet way about Prashun ji.

In the days and months after Indrani invited me over many times to take my mind off the grief I was feeling. I came to know the family very well and kept occupied by cooking for them and eventually became closer to this group of people. This connection and the time spent together was so helpful in such a painful period of my life, where it felt like a tsunami had come, taken away my dearest friend and was engulfing me.

TIME TO SAY FAREWELL

Chatterjee Uncle never predicted anyone's death, except in two cases.

Once he shared with me about Prashun ji, "He will be fine until he is 73 years." This was the exact age my friend passed away.

Another time, in 1999, I noticed that Chatterjee Uncle's health started getting down. I asked him, "Kaku, are you going to the doctors to find out what is happening to your body?" He answered, "Please, do not worry, I will be fine another 10 years; for 10 years nobody can do anything to me." Right after 10 years, in 2009, he fell from his bed and, despite having treatment, passed away at the age of 72.

During the years of our interaction Chatterjee Uncle gave me an overall guideline of my life. Still, even after his death, I was following the predictions he had given me when he was alive. For example, he told me that I should never give up my painting side whatever happens. Also, he kept asking me to sign my works. I thought he was just making fun of me.

But then, when we were shut down due to pandemic, I have created 179 paintings only during the year 2020. Now some of these works are in private collections, and soon I am having my fifth exhibition.

CHATTERJEE UNCLE— AMAZING ANECDOTES AND PREDICTIONS

All this time we have been concentrating on my life story where the influence of astrology and my astrologer was so remarkable. Now I would like to take a different approach and share some other predictions of Chatterjee Uncle which came true for others and which I personally witnessed.

Chatterjee Uncle had a friend named Mr. Sharma, a Marwari businessman who he had known for a long time. When his son got married, although the family was well liked, issues developed when the daughter-in-law could not get pregnant. Uncle made her chart and said it will happen. "She will have to wait a little longer," he said, "it will be a baby boy." Mr. Sharma told his daughter-in-law that Uncle said they must be patient. Years went by. Then again Mr. Sharma asked Uncle, "What is happening, we still don't have a baby, how much more waiting will be there?" Then Chatterjee Uncle said, "From the time you asked me for my view of the chart almost ten years ago, I saw that the waiting could be this length of time. Don't give up your hope." Then exactly ten years after that reading, a baby boy was born. Mr. Sharma was so grateful, he sent flowers, sweets, and huge baskets of gifts to Chatterjee Uncle's house. This again demonstrates his tremendous power of prediction.

~ ~ ~

When my father wanted my elder sister to get married, he looked far and wide for a match. During this process of some weeks, Chatterjee Uncle came to our house. At that time my Didi* was home, so he looked at Didi's palm. My Mom provided her birth timing, so he could do a chart. Mom was very serious about doing her chart because she knew my father was looking for a groom for her. A lot of families had been contacting my father about my sister. Chatterjee Uncle looked at the palm and birth info and made his way home shortly after this important visit. He came back a few days later with the chart. Chatterjee Uncle asked what the rush was to get her married. My Mother replied, "This is a perfect time for her to get married and start a family. She is of that age." Chatterjee Uncle said, "I see good academics in her chart. She can further her studies, especially in

---

* *Elder sister in Bengali*

language. Just don't rush. Let her study." He asked my mother if it would be possible to back out of the preliminary conversations with the family. My Mom told my father what Chatterjee Uncle had said, but my father wouldn't listen and went ahead and gave a positive word to the potential new husband's family. So the marriage took place with the family and their son. The groom's intentions in the marriage were to get a job at my father's company. When this job placement did not happen, he turned on my sister, eventually berating her and repeatedly accusing her of being crazy. The marriage intent, it seems, had nothing to do with my sister. The husband's family then attempted to kick her out of their house by saying she had mental issues. My sister came back home after just seven days. Baba went through the entire lawsuit that the family had against my sister saying that she was crazy. Baba won the case, but it took six long years to process. Then, nine years later, my sister received another marriage offer from a man who turned out to be abusive and was a womanizer. Again she returned home. For this time as well Chatterjee Uncle also had warned that unless the future husband's family had land and properties, she should not get married. While looking at my sister's charts, he told my Mom, "I don't really see a success in matrimony for either Mala or your eldest daughter. Be very careful about their marriage possibilities. The rest two girls though will both be fine with their respective marriages." After 30 or 40 years, I can see that just what he had said came true. He knew the heaviness of this statement about me and my sister and its impact though he said it simply. My sister's two marriages both broke and I myself never married. Our other two siblings did have good marriages just as he had stated.

~ ~ ~

Chatterjee Uncle did Prashun ji's chart. From time to time after that in the years that followed, he asked after him. Chatterjee Uncle knew that his health would become a problem and tried to also prepare my mind for this aspect. One day he asked and I said he was okay except for a funny cough. He then said, "Ask him to be careful on an "uthan"*, or long porch and front of the house." "His house or uthan?" I asked. "No, any kind of porch area. He won't be killed by this, he will be survive, he will be saved (in Bengali, "phara"), but ask him to be a little careful," Chatterjee Uncle replied. A few days later, Prashun ji was robbed in front of his home—two rings, wallet, gold chain with a coin that had been gifted, necklace, watch. The thieves took those things and beat him and left. They made him lie in uthan and count to 100. The next day Prashun ji came to check on me and Jethima and asked, "Do you see anything different with me?" I didn't notice, but Jethima noticed

---

* *Driveway in Bengali*

right away, "Where are your chains, your rings?" He said, "She is right, I was robbed yesterday."

~ ~ ~

Chatterjee Uncle predicted in 1979 by looking at my hand and my chart that my father would soon be giving up his job. At that time, my father was one of the top managers in the British Airways' office in Kolkata. Chatterjee Uncle didn't know my father and had no idea about his work or background, but by looking at my hand this understanding came to him. No one could have imagined this, especially my mother. She did not believe it even when I told her of Chatterjee Uncle's vision. In about three weeks' time though, she came to know that he had already given up his job without telling anyone, taking early retirement right then and there. Chatterjee Uncle had also predicted that my father would be a changed man after that. This is so true, and we all witnessed this directly. He mellowed and his temper became less intense. We also noticed that he somehow seemed to age more quickly without being so active and involved with a job. Later he would demonstrate doubt about things that before he had taken for granted during the years while he was working.

~ ~ ~

Chatterjee Uncle looked at my younger sister Tutul's chart after my Mother requested him to, as she was apprehensive about her future husband. Tutul had always been determined to marry someone based on her own choice and feelings and without any consultation with the family. Chatterjee Uncle said, "Whoever Tutul chooses, that person will develop some sort of deficiency in the body." He said he could not tell exactly what it would be. Later, when I was in Kolkata in 1985, I noticed that her husband limped when he walked, reflecting just what Chatterjee Kaku had predicted.

~ ~ ~

In the year 1985, as he looked at my chart, Chatterjee Uncle told me that in five years' time some weird person would come and disturb me a lot. He said he was uncomfortable with this. He said, "This is one problem that will come to you even during what is otherwise a very successful period." He added, "This person will test your clarity of perception and patience as he is someone who likes to play games being not what he seems." After five years passed, I wrote to Chatterjee Uncle saying, "I think your prediction was not correct as no strange person has arrived to trouble me." He just simply replied by saying that I should be careful. Later that year (1990) in March this man finally popped up. He began to stalk me with constant phone calls. He was following me home from various locations and leaving prank messages on my answering machine. I was miserable, not knowing what to do and not being able to predict the man's erratic behavior.

I called Chatterjee Uncle and he said I had a few months more of suffering. I told him I could not call the police as it would affect my reputation since I was well known person within the community. It would create a scandal with me looking bad, instead of this stalker. Chatterjee Uncle did more calculations of my chart at my urging and told me that by the 25th of November this bad yog would dissipate. I would be leaving behind this period and the kind of difficulty that I had been experiencing. And it happened the way I was told

~ ~ ~

Interestingly, I met someone in 1981 in L.A. who was a student at UCLA and was a guest like me in someone's home while she was studying. In a very short period of time we became friends with this woman, who was close to my age and also staying in another person's house as a guest while she too studied. Sree was blamed by her host who thought she had stolen one of her pieces of jewelry. It was an heirloom from her grandmother. Her auntie wrote to Sree's father that her jewelry was missing, and she said that Sree was the one who stole. Sree said this was a wrong perception, that she came from a beautiful family and stealing was not in her nature. Sree was very shook up about this and shared her very sensitive story about the host's accusation with me. She asked me if I knew any astrologer who might be able to help her understand. I said I did and could recommend someone. I, of course, immediately thought of Chatterjee Uncle. I asked him if he could prepare and read Sree's chart for her. He found out from this that she was not guilty, that the accusation was a false one and a manufactured plan. Chatterjee Uncle could see in the chart though, that Sree would reconcile with the host soon. He said it would be proved that Sree was not guilty. "I am an astrologer and studied the subject but am not God. I am trying my level best to give you the answer. She herself will find her own jewelry." He continued to reflect, "I am seeing a good relationship with this lady. It will continue as such." Chatterjee Uncle told Sree that she should go back to the house and stay, and that eventually the situation would be resolved. "The rest in life that might happen after this", he added, "we don't know, and we leave to God, but please don't worry, she will apologize. These small problems are in your chart."

This is exactly what happened. Sree went back to the house, and the host later apologized, saying she had found the piece of jewelry in her garage. She said that she realized she was blaming others for taking things without doing the proper search for lost items. Their relationship was in better harmony after this.

~ ~ ~

A major famous artist who was my father's very close friend, like a brother, told him that I was as a daughter to him he would be ready to support. He said, "Tell Mala to ask me if she needs any financial help while here in the U.S." This artist was a second father to me, a role model, an idol I worshipped all my life. Once he was in some mental stress and confusion having taken a wrong medicine, and things suddenly went awry. Because of my Chatterjee Uncle and his astrology, he was significantly helped in managing these experiences. Chatterjee Uncle did the chart for this artist, mentioning to him that he would experience some trauma in his life in the areas of his profession, organizational work, and health. Chatterjee Uncle wrote these things down very clearly, "You will have problems with your colleagues and people who are working under you. You will have problems there but still, you should try to keep harmony with these individuals. Do not distrust them, you must try and trust them. They are not your enemies. Additionally, the next time when you come to India, likely you will need to be careful, especially with your money." Since many of the points in the chart were negative, this artist had some difficulties hearing this and said that everything was wrong. "My birth time is not sure," he had said. But when he went to India just after this interaction, he called me and surprisingly asked me to give him the number of Chatterjee Uncle. He would eventually call him every other month to receive his guidance, which had a positive influence, including a message and prediction that his son would keep his name shining with music.

~ ~ ~

Mr. Krishna was looking for a bride while he was studying in Los Angeles. He was impressed with an eligible girl he met, and their signs matched as did their age. Both the families also believed in the same guru. From the outside it looked like an amazing match (called "Rajyotok" in Bengali). They liked each other on the phone also. Mr. Krishna wanted to see Binodini and experience talking to her in person, and going out for a day. It looked very promising. They were both focused on each other and enthusiastic to meet. When they were getting more serious, and when he wanted to make his next visit and talk to the family, the girl's side happened to have the same idea, but something went wrong. From the girl's side, her mother started pushing the issue of marriage saying, "Don't come now, come after four months." Four months became six months, and it so happened that in the meantime Mr. Krishna was very interested in doing his chart with Chatterjee Uncle. At this point, he did not know anything about the relationship Mr. Krishna was developing. He looked at the chart carefully and said, "Please give a little time, I really don't know quite yet what to say. From the outside the chart can look just right, but something is off and I am not sure what it is." This perception occurred to him after looking at her chart as well. He could sense there was a roadblock somewhere. Mr. Krishna was very disappointed. He was very committed to and focused on this relationship developing. Chatterjee Uncle though remained skeptical about the match, repeatedly saying, "Something is not right. Please give this some more time." In a couple of months there was a message from Binodini's mother, saying "We are not sure of the marriage, let's not talk about it yet." Then Krishna found out that Binodini had some health issues and would first need to heal from this before any kind of marriage could take place. The marriage kept getting continuously delayed and the families felt it might be best to conclude the preparations for marriage as it wasn't working out. Chatterjee Uncle asked Mr. Krishna to consider other possibilities for a wife. Mr. Krishna traveled to India and was introduced to five different girls. Chatterjee Uncle made a prediction here too when Mr. Krishna went to visit him in India. "Your destiny is overseas and not in India. It will be fruitful for you and you will benefit in the long run." Mr. Krishna was feeling disappointed with this perception as he always wanted to remain in India. Among the five girls he had met, it turned out that he liked one of them in particular. While he was preparing to get married to her, some issues came up with his eyes and they decided to postpone the marriage. Around this time, Chatterjee Uncle called me about Mr. Krishna's chart. He said he noticed that the sun sign in the chart was weak and it left Chatterjee Uncle wondering what this might mean. He said, "There is something with Mr. Krishna's sun line ("Robi Dasha"). I didn't see him wearing glasses in my initial vision of him. Is something the matter with his eyes?" After a few days, I decided to follow up with Mr. Krishna, "Is everything okay with your eyes? You don't usually wear glasses as you do now." Mr. Krishna said, "That man is a genius. I have been going to doctors, and I wear contact lenses, so people don't know about my eye problems. The pupils of my eyes are getting pointed so in another few years I could have difficulty seeing at all. It is a birth defect." Mr. Krishna then had to postpone his immediate plans for marriage among the women he had met, and travel back to the U.S. for some eye treatment from UCLA. After this treatment, he went back to India and married one of the women he had met before he had the eye issue and the need for treatment. This marriage was a positive one, and it created a beautiful family. Ten years later Krishna's eyes deteriorated so much that he needed an eye transplant. He always wanted to go back to India but needed to stay for the medical expertise and efficiency of treatment in the U.S.

Whenever Mr. Krishna looks back and thinks about Chatterjee Uncle's predictions, he remembers how annoyed he had felt about having to return to the U.S. He had also thought he never wanted to study medicine. "Now, though I am approaching 50," he would say, "I can see how I have a happy family with two beautiful daughters and wife and am a successful doctor. I have certainly benefited from the medical expertise and efficiency of this country. But I am very grateful for the predictions of Chatterjee Uncle and also quite amazed. How could I have known all this then?"

~ ~ ~

I know of a brilliant pianist whose recognition was not what it should be, given his enormous musicianship. Chatterjee Uncle prepared his chart. I did not tell him this musician's gender and instead asked him about his financial situation and his recognition as an artist. Chatterjee Uncle asked me then why I wasn't telling him whether this was a man or a woman. I said, "Uncle, I am particularly hiding it from you." "This is a very tough question, that's not right," he replied, "You should tell me." He continued, "I see a wonderful change in his work and he will reach a higher level in the years after he is 59. It will be a turning point. He will also become very comfortable financially for the rest of his life. A little struggle will be there until that time including financial loss. He will need to be careful handling money. And, regarding gender, if this person is a man, he is someone who will always be attracted to men physically. If a woman, she would like to be attached mentally or romantically with a woman." Even though Chatterjee Uncle was not aware of the possibility that homosexuality existed, he saw this in the pianist's chart. And as it turned out, exactly at the age of 59 he was chosen by a renowned composer and music director of Bollywood films to work with him. This was pivotal, as this pianist had just lost his job as a music teacher at a college. By 60 years of age, he was called by the acclaimed music director to teach and perform in Singapore. Chatterjee Uncle had warned him as he had read in his chart about a financial loss. Later I came to know that he had lost approximately 3 lakhs of rupees to someone he was in a relationship with. Years later though, he has his own home, a car and a wonderful job at the conservatory of a great music composer. Just after eight years at this job, stability in his home and his career all happened. It was just after his 59th year. Chatterjee Uncle was also correct about his gender leanings as he was someone who identified as gay. I had deliberately not told Chatterjee Uncle how remarkable a pianist he was and with what feeling he could bring out of his instrument! I asked Chatterjee Uncle if he sensed the instrument this man played and he said, "I don't know, except that I can see that this artist is very creative, and the instrument he plays has something to do with hammers." Later when I spoke with my friend about this prediction for him, he said that Chatterjee Uncle was absolutely right. The earliest piano, he explained, was known at one time as a hammer dulcimer and the modern piano today also has small hammers for each string and piano key! Yes again, another miracle prediction by Chatterjee Uncle.

~ ~ ~

A friend was having a midlife crisis, and Chatterjee Uncle was asked to help and do his chart as he was finding himself restless and having affairs outside his marriage and not sure of what he was really doing. Chatterjee Uncle said of his newest affair, "Your timing with this situation is not good, so we will still have to see what will happen. But I think what I tell you will eventually bring some satisfaction. With whatever number of days you have left in this affair, you should be very careful with this relationship. You will be hearing some news from her soon. My suggestion is to stay away. Your life will be ruined if you try to stay with her, you will regret it. I don't think it is a good connection for you for your future. It is not going to work out. Give some more time to adjust things with your wife. I know what the problems are there. You so have a much better time coming, just hold onto the ground." Then he asked my friend, "You have three children, right?" My friend conveyed the response to me which I then shared with Chatterjee Uncle, "I just have two children, a son and a daughter." My friend called me later that night and said full of emotion, "Mala ji, after I went home I spoke with my wife about Chatterjee Uncle's question about children. Together we remembered how we had made a decision many years earlier to have an abortion, just before our marriage. We were sad to do that and even to this day we regret it. We were so young, and we were shy to let our families and community know we were pregnant before our marriage and had no money. I had no job." Later I found out that the woman he was having an affair with told him she was off to Hawaii as she had begun an affair now with someone else. She flatly said goodbye and put the phone down. My friend and his family went on to stay together and over time cultivated a deeper love. They created a home over the years and their family stayed solid, with many grandchildren. Chatterjee Uncle's advice and insights had proven to be so true.

AFTERWORD

I am always praising, appreciating, and being amazed by my Chatterjee Uncle, due to the many sensitive and accurate predictions he made throughout his lifetime. I must admit that these changed my life totally. They made me reach my goal. Still, at the end of the day, I don't want to recommend that anyone slavishly follow any astrological predictions. In other words, what I am trying to establish here is that if you would like to believe or follow the beautiful science of astrology, I would strongly recommend that you look for a real astrologer who has studied the subject thoroughly. And secondly, if at any time of your life, you feel the need for astrological guidance, please, don't blindly go for it, you must do your karma (hard work) and take responsibility for your life choices, and then combine this with the guidance you receive. Chatterjee Uncle repeated it many times. "I am not God. Never accept what I say without reflection. You do your karma, then you will see something come. Listen to your heart. Have faith in yourself and in God." And to me specifically he said, "You will have major success in the later part of your career."

In this book we are talking about a phenomenal astrologer who himself did not realize how good he was in this subject and how much he could assist someone's life through this science. His extraordinary knowledge, borne of years of study, was combined with a strong ethical nature, deep intuition and genuine humility.

Chatterjee Uncle always mentioned that no bad or harmful feelings should be directed at those that have disturbed one. He would say, "I only alert you to this because that particular influence is not good for your journey/chart."

Also, he was a very generous human being, he never asked anything in return, it was unconditional giving. He didn't expect anything, even our acceptance. He offered his service out of love and compassion and with imperative that came from caring of a person. He shared not only his knowledge and insight, but also material things. Sometimes he would be near someone he knew or a stranger when suddenly he sensed that a stone or gem was needed to help their life situation, he would take off his own ring from his hand and give it. Like one man couldn't afford marriage of his daughter. Chatterjee Uncle took an expensive stone out of his ring right at the railway station and presented to that man so he could provide a proper future for the girl.

But the irony is that this same multi-talented individual did not find success in his own career. He struggled to create a livelihood throughout his life. He was so talented in many areas, but his very trusting nature and the financial difficulties that ensued had psychological consequences. Nothing clicked or came to fruition. Even no one knew of his deep skill in astrology because he did not formally take it as a profession. Chatterjee Uncle never charged any money for his astrological readings. It was his *nesha* (passion and love) and not his *pesha* (livelihood of necessity). In later years some friends, who saw my success with his predictions and also needed help from him, offered some financial help in exchange for his guidance. But he never asked for this, any funds always came from their goodwill and as a way to honor his generosity and expertise.

Whatever happened in my life, he was always giving positive input saying, "Do not worry (*chinta karben na*), things are going to work out." It was his mantra.

My gratitude to the Almighty. I realize now how blessed I was to have this extraordinary person and astrologer—someone who was just like family—both supporting and guiding me throughout my life. He came as a gift at a very crucial time. Although those around me could not recognize this, he was like an actual angel at the very moment when I needed him the most. My life's circumstances and disappointments, along with the emotional vulnerabilities that come with having an artistic nature, can make it difficult to choose the best steps forward. At one point, I was so lost and needed clear vision and support. Luckily, he appeared with his input and depth of insight, helping to make my life move forward in the most meaningful way.

ABOUT THE AUTHOR

MALA GANGULY is a distinguished Indian virtuoso vocalist, awwarded with the epithet "Nightingale of California." Pioneering the usage of Indian Classical Music in mainstream American commercials for Nike, and the CBS movie *The Christmas Box*, Mala Ganguly performs throughout North America as a touring and recording artist. Her vast repertoire includes Bhajans, Geets, Ghazals, Thumris, Bollywood film songs, and all styles of Bengali music. Widely acclaimed for her extraordinary vocal skill, Mala Ganguly is especially appreciated for her sweet timbre, flexibility, spontaneous complex vocal improvisation, and technical virtuosity. As a SAG/AFTRA performer, she works regularly as a composer and singer for Hollywood movies, TV jingles, voice overs, and fusion music. Recently, Mala gave voice to such films and television seriess as *Mission Impossible 4*, *Big Bang Theory*, *Eat Pray Love*, and *The Most Fearless*.

Mala Ganguly is the founder of The Surmala Music Academy which is dedicated to furthering the fine arts of India. Her original artwork has been exhibited in the Laguna Beach Arts Festival and Monrovia Arts Festival in San Francisco and Los Angeles.

Since 1995 she has been working as a vocalist, actor, lyricist, and composer for Hollywood movies and television.

www.malaganguly.com

malaganguly@yahoo.com

https://youtu.be/DhIayGKlPTs

https://youtu.be/QliurHUykJI

www.ingramcontent.com/pod-product-compliance
Lightning Source LLC
Chambersburg PA
CBHW070553030426
42337CB00016B/2474